My Chains Are Broken:
The Obstacles of Overcoming Drug Addiction

My Chains Are Broken:
The Obstacles of Overcoming Drug Addiction

Antonette Brown

With Editor,

Kisha Battle Houston

UNOME PUBLISHERS
2023

Scriptural references were provided by https://www.biblegateway.com.

First Printing: 2023

ISBN 978-1-312-65594-2
Imprint: Lulu.com

Unome Publishers
Owings Mills, Maryland

www.unomepublishers.com

Dedication

To my editor, friends, family, my pastor, my church and my narcotics anonymous support group.

Thank you. Without your support and patience, I would have never achieved my dream.

To you, O God, I give the praise.

Deliverance is mine saith the Lord.

Contents

Acknowledgements

I acknowledge my Pastor Chad and his wife, Lady T, Elder Travis, my church family, United Church of Jesus Christ Apostolic, my father in the gospel Bishop J.B. Thornton and wife Daisy Thornton, my natural family, my N.A. family and a host of friends. I'd like to acknowledge the most important person in my life, my best friend who made this all possible, Jesus Christ. To Him be the glory for the great things He has done. To God be the glory. I acknowledge my editor and publisher, Mrs. Kisha Battle Houston of Unome Publishers who found favor in me.

Foreword

Truth is the foundation of my interactions.

I am anchored in truthfulness. When communicating with others, I am as truthful as possible while still remaining respectful. I try to steer away from situations that would require me to be deceitful. I live a fine life as a good person. Therefore, I am free from the burden of being forced to shimmy my way out of situations without being truthful.

If I do something wrong, I admit to my mistakes. If I am faced with a situation where taking the easy way out would include lying, I always choose the road which bases itself on honesty. There are consequences for every action; therefore I live my life while walking on a path that I feel comfortable with.

There are a few exceptions where I may not speak the entire truth to spare the feelings of another. I am aware of the fact that some situations are better off when I find something positive to say, instead.

Living a truthful life means adhering to my obligations, being a trustworthy person, and being straightforward in my interactions with others. It does not mean using the truth as a battering ram to assault or criticize.

Today, I speak honestly and with integrity. I know right from wrong, and I use my moral compass to help me base my interactions with others on truth.

Self-Reflection Questions:

1. Are my interactions based on honesty and integrity?

2. Do I know how to choose my moments to speak honestly?

3. Am I confident enough to speak honestly in most situations?

Introduction

What do you do to experience peace? Prayer, reading and meditating on God's word showers, hair done, nails done, and baths. Nail shop, feet care. Affirmations and reading.

I need to trust God in the areas of my career, my finances, my healthcare, my hair, my clothes, etc.

What way I deceived myself about my own sin is by saying that lying is a small sin is by saying that lying is a small sin when all unrighteousness is sin. There is no little sins or big sins. Sin is wickedness against God himself.

God's peace isn't an absence of conflict, but rather a deep sense of security even in distress. A peace that passes all understanding and protects our hearts and minds in the midst of the most difficult of circumstances. Thou (God) will keep us in complete peace when our minds are stayed on His word (thee) because He trusted in thee. Thank you Jesus.

I find that when I am trusting in my own abilities instead of trusting God and His leading; I feel deep unrest in my heart. Sometimes I feel anxious, but I think on the word. Take no thought for your life. Be anxious for naught. I will and am talking and taking care of you. My affliction God delivered me from my afflictions. He redeemed me from the bondage of sin, free the world from the god of this world. God heard my cry by reasons of Satan- the accuser of the brethren. He knew my sorrows.

God is still in the process of healing me. I've been on medicine since 1980. I was diagnosed with bipolar depression, but God let me know that I just had issues and that I was traumatized. Now everybody in addiction or addicts are diagnosed with bipolar or depression or anxiety. Mental illness is running crazy. Satan is crazy so he wants us to be like him instead of Jesus. I will be made whole by my faith. God knew that it is time to heal me so I can share my testimony. I refused to take the medicine for years because I didn't believe I was sick. I believe that I had childhood scars that need therapy. I was spiritually sick and mentally sick. God raised me from the dead- for He is the God of the living and not the dead.

God showed me that when I am in His will, I don't feel unworthy or dirty. I don't want to have sex with the devil (men). God showed me that when I am in His will, I don't want to have sex (with men) because He is my spiritual husband. He doesn't want me to cheat or cause Him to become jealous. When I am in self and in my own will, I want pleasure, and sex only to support my habit. I don't feel clean on the inside when I'm in self-will. I was a prostitute selling my body for a hit of crack only. God cleaned me up on the inside His blood. He allows me to clean the outside with soap and water.

God cleans my soul with His blood. He gave me the oil of gladness over all my brokenness. My first experience with drugs was in the home at the age of 9 years old. My first drug was sex. I was born prematurely at 6 pounds. Me and my brother slept in dresser drawers. My mother was comforting and loving. My father was mean and aggressive. He fought my mother. We would fight him. I remember when Allen, who is my gay brother, bust my father with a vase in his head.

In my home was arguing, fighting and poverty. My mother's mother told her not to marry my father. She (my mother) married him as a ticket to get away from her mother. She suffered for it. And he was dysfunctional. He was in the home but not emotionally there, just physically. He showed his girls no love or affection. We received no hugs or kisses. No allowance. We were poor.

My father molested me. He fondled and stroked me with his person. He was an evil man. Because of him molesting me, I became pessimistic and sexual with a lot of men in the home (foster) first. I slept with me in the home. Black and white. The home was beautiful. A baseball field, a recreation center, a pool, and a basketball court. But the newness wore off and I became homesick. I longed to be with my mother.

This was the first feeling of abandonment. My mother took sick, and she couldn't take care of us, so we were placed in foster care. Two of my siblings did not come but the rest of us did. My mother gave birth to ten children, six girls and four boys. One brother died from renal failure. He went to N.A.

After I left the foster home, we lived in a five-bedroom house where me and my sister stayed in our own room. My mother was in the back room. My other siblings paired into their own rooms too. It was there when my addiction took over. There was a counselor at the foster home. He was also a drug dealer and had me selling marijuana when I was twenty joints in the bag not like today.

I took LSD, pills, and Valiums. I remember knocking a wall out when my mother hit me with a bar of soap. I would steal her money to buy drugs and she knew it was me, but she loved me so much. It wasn't really until I attended Towson University that I went from being a Honors student to a college dropout. I didn't understand that I was sick, either mentally, physically, psychologically, or spiritually in sin. And my issues and my pain spiraled from there.

I remember that I had a nervous breakdown after enlisting in the Navy and as time passed not dealing with my bipolar depression and traumatic stress, I eventually lost control after the death of my mother. That begins my story in Narcotics Anonymous, my step program, my journaling, and the healing from my pain. I can only pray that as you read my treatment progress, my spiritual journey through biblical teachings, prayer, and meditation, that you can begin to understand the difficulties and obstacles overcoming addiction. It's not just about drug addiction but what led to the addiction that we fail to recognize, accept, and handle in our own way.

Instead of pressing through the trauma with persistent counseling, we numb ourselves, push it down and store our pain away. This is only a portion of my story but it's the most important part of my journey. I have been given a second chance to heal from the pain, to leave behind emotional sin, to forgive my trespasses and my trespassers as God have given us mercy. My life is no accident. I am not a mistake. I have been put on this earth to share my story as it may prove enlightening to other addicts suffering with emotional pain and suffering.

Know that you do not have to suffer alone. Narcotics Anonymous has been an important part of my recovery along with my faith in the Lord Jesus Christ. God knows your heart and has a plan for you too. Seek Him in your quest for healing and He will bring you out of it if you surrender your old life to Him. Today is your day to have a positive influence, make a change and break the chains holding you. My chains are broken. It's your time to heal too.

My Journals: Treatment Plan

December 12, 2020

On a Saturday, my last day I used drugs, I had six dollars, and I didn't have the desire to use. I knew then that a power greater than me was working again.

Today is Sunday. Today was a quiet day. I woke up at 5:30 AM. I woke up in a cold sweat. I am detoxing and withdrawing the crack I put in my body. I took a hot shower [sat?] and was up until twelve in the morning in my room reading Recovery and Relapse. I read it more than one time so I can get an understanding of where I went off track. Why did I relapse this time? I learnt that my relapse wasn't an accident, but a choice I made - really simple. I stop working on my program on a daily basis. I stop calling Towanda who is my guide. A sponsor is a guide. I stop listening to the recovering addicts on Zoom. I disconnected from the fellowship.

It took courage for me to come back. I couldn't save my face and my ass at the same time. I lost contact with other recovering addicts. I was blame my mental illness and my past for my using. I no longer do that. I forgot the troubles that drugs cause when you pick them up. I forget of I don't pick the up they can't get in me. Treatment is reminding me of the information that I already had. But I lost the information because I used. When you use, you lose.

December 16, 2020

I am in treatment.

I am feeling depressed because of the negative things Dawn said. She doesn't understand my disease of addiction or my mental illness. Satan used her to shoot his fiery darts at me. My pattern is that I will stop taking my medicine then I pick up the crack. This time when I relapse I, first of all, disconnected from my sponsors, from my outside help (my therapist and psychiatrist.); I stop listening to the recovering addicts on Zoom; I stop using all my N.A. tools and information.

I can't understand the baffling, cunning and insidious nature of this disease. I am ready to change my environment. I want to be in a healthier environment. I need to go back to praying and reading my Bible. I am glad I am in treatment because I am back on my medicine.

Maybe I need some to give me my medicine. Sometimes I do good, then I become irresponsible and stop taking it.

This has been my pattern.

Maybe I shouldn't live by myself. I don't know. I have my own room. It is snow out on the ground. It is miserable being sick and not take your medicine. You would think many times that I been in the hospital I would have learned to take it. To be truthful it can be a struggle taking it. I do good for a while then I'll stop.

I want to change people, places, and things. I want to stay on my medicine and not get off it. I want to stay out of the hospitals. I remember my clean day.

December 22, 2020

God woke me up at 5:30.

We took our vitals and then we drank coffee. I felt the effects of the medicine. I was drowsiness and dizziness. I shared in group how I felt. I laid in bed until wore off. Today in group we talk about depression. I learned that it is not that I am lazy, and lack of motivation and ambition is one of the traits of my depression. I learned that. not taking care of my hygiene is one of the traits of my depression. I learned that eating bananas helps me to gain potassium. I learned that I could start off with a voluntary job - not doing too many hours.

The nurse's name was Margie. She was really professional, and she knew what she was talking about. I am looking forward to going to Gardenia's. I shared my pain in group, and it went away.

Thank God, I can say the Serenity Prayer and start my day over. I'm glad I have a program as long as I follow the N.A. program. I never have to has or fear.

December 23, 2020, 8:20 PM

I just finished eating snacks. God woke me up at 5:00 AM. I had to urinate then I went back to bed. The headaches that I was having went away because they took me off the Benadryl. I talked to Towanda today. She was helping her still-suffering addict brother Charles. I leave to go into a treatment rehab called *Gardenia*. I am extremely excited. I have been restored through another recovering addict - the recovering addiction treatment.

Some of the counselors I found out why I keep picking. I thought I couldn't stay clean on my own without sponsorship and the program I stop working my program on a daily basis. I learned that my relapse was not an accident, but we are given a choice. I chose to pick up. It is that simple.

I learned that this program is a simple program, but I keep comprehension it. I learned that the illusion has to be shattered - that I can't stay clean on my own. I learned that staying clean must be my first priority. If not I won't get the job, the car, the house, or nothing until I make staying clean come first. The racing thoughts have stopped because of the Prolixin. My sleep has improved. I take showers again. My appetite is back because they gave me a vitamin. I sleep on clean sheets and a pillowcase. My pressure medicine makes me urinate. I have been drinking plenty of water to flush the medicine. She lowered my sleeping medicine to 25 mg. I was having cold and hot flashes. That is getting better I am not in Christmas spirit, but I am not knocking those who are.

December 25, 2020

I am in an excellent mood. My medicines are working. I am in a stable mood. I am sleeping better and eating better. The food in CR Inc. is excellent. The water of the showers is hot. The bed is comfortable. I am excited about going to Gardenia on Monday. No more co stupa toon or migraine headaches.

The therapist give me i formation on my mental illness. My diagnosis is Bipolar Manic Depression. I learned the sum of my mental illness.

Extreme mood shifts - I have trouble managing everyday life tasks at school, work, or maintaining relationships.

The medicine helps me maintain my symptoms. Here are the symptoms: **spending sprees, unprotected sex, and drug use.**

When I am in my depression,

- **I experience deep sadness and hopelessness.**
- **Loss of energy**
- **Lack of energy**
- **Lack of interest in activities I once enjoyed**
- **Periods of too little or too much sleep**
- **suicidal thoughts**
- **I experienced an emotional high**

I learned that there are three types of bipolar: bipolar I, Bipolar II, and Cyclothymia. Bipolar II last at least two weeks. Right now, because if the medicine, my mood is stable, and I must keep it that way.

December 26, 2020

In my room. I just got up from prayer. The Lord woke me up at 3:13am. I had to go to the bathroom. I was sweating again. Last night, I took off my sweater. It is hot in this room. Thank God for the heat. It reminded me and my boyfriend when we were sleeping in a cold empty house with a bed and lots of cover. Because of my detoxing. I would get cold chills then hot chills. I ask for more covers. Last night I slept under one cover and was still hot. I didn't go back to bed this morning because I drank two cups of coffee instead of one. I usually drink one cup. I worked on a word puzzle. The nurse here gave us a gift bag and one of the counselors.

Tyler gave us candy. I've been having a sweet tooth even though I don't have any teeth. I have been able to eat my food. My favorite dishes are pancakes and sausage. Another favorite dish is cheese steak. We get a lot of food. A lot of food is wasted here. They can't save it, so they throw it away. Some people hate wasting food.

My bowels is moving better. I'm still excited about going to Gardenia. I was given a medicine box to keep up with taking my medicine. My mood is good. I took my medicine. The mark on my nose share I burned is still there and the burn on my thumb is still there reminding me of the devastation of my active addiction. I tried calling my sponsor this morning but couldn't reach her. She was probably still in bed. Sometimes I sleep too little or too much. But I thank God for his grace and mercy. Now I am about to read recovery and relapse.

December 30, 2020

I am home from treatment. I got home yesterday. I was supposed to go to Gardenia, but it will not open until January 4, 2022. We waited for a while. I was a little disappointed because I was looking forward to going. But I had to accept the things I cannot change.

I blamed my case manager.

Today is Wednesday. I was reading. Today I cleaned out both of my closets of all the clothes that I'm not wearing. I got rid of them. I took my meds this morning. I tried to call my therapist, but she was not in.

Gratitude List

Here are the things I'm grateful for:
A relationship with God
My meds (recovery)
My joy
My family
Sponsorship
Water and soap
A bed to sleep in
A roof over my head
My prayer life
N.A. and the literature
The use and activity of all my limbs (even pain)
That I can feel again - that happiness/peace (contentment)
The scriptures
Friends and family
Heat
Sleep

It is cold outside. I'll probably stay in today and read my N.A. literature and tonight I'll call Towanda and take a hot bath and soak in some Epsom salt.

January 1, 2021, 7:15 AM

God woke me up at 7:15.

The first thing I did was take my medicine. I spent my New Year in a meeting with Towanda. 2020 was a rough year but I got through it. I am glad i survived my relapse. It was nothing but God's grace and mercy and his favor. It was not my doing. I'm mad at Keith for wanting to buy me lunch or dinner. I refused. He was happy for me that I was clean. My mood is good. I called Dawn. I haven't heard from her since I been in treatment. Carol either. I miss them.

January 2, 2021, 8:45 AM

It was a fire this morning around three or four in the morning. I was in a deep sleep. I tried to get away from everybody, especially the practicing addicts. I have to separate myself from them. Be cordial, but not partake in their lifestyle.

I engage in thoroughly cleaning my apartment. I clean my walls where the maintenance men had left marks on my doors and walls. I prayed today and read literature and some devotions from the scriptures. I even read my daily bread.

My mood was excellent. I talked to my friend Aaron. He was happy to hear from me. I reconnected with him. He is someone who wants to help me in my recovery. I have a sugar craving, but I have to be careful. Because of my disease, if I use self-control instead of moderation I can use without. a drink or drug.

January 3, 2021

Yesterday I cleaned my apartment and talked to Stephanie and Towanda and Aaron. I read my scriptures on suffering in I Peter.

Yesterday The disease was active on me in the form of fear and anxiety God lead me to say the serenity prayer until I feel better. I prayed the Lord's prayer also. I gave up cigarettes. My clean day is January 2, 2021. My clean day when the obsession and compulsion was lifted not to use drugs. (crack, cocaine, alcohol).

Tricks, steal, prostitution all lifting. I gave up the energy drinks yesterday. I pour my last two down the drain.

I got rid of all my ash trays and threw my lighter away.

It is a mind over matter thing. Half the battle is getting your mind set and your body will catch up. I ate 20 nuggets and a large fry. A large, sweet tea. I need to change my eating habits. I am going to eat more fruits and vegetables, apple sauce, tuna fish, fish, salmon, green bean, hotdogs, and salads.

January 7, 2021, 5:10 AM

God woke me up at 5:10 AM.

I had a good sleep because of my medicine. I am in treatment. An orientation meaning I must stay in my room until my COVID is verified. I ask God to get me up earlier, so I won't miss my morning meds. My roommate, Regina, left and she stole my cocoa butter.

Today will be a good day. I hope we will have group, but because of the COVID, we haven't had any groups. Things have been shut down. This is not like CR Inc. The food is terrible, but I don't complain; some people don't get a meal. Thank God for Jesus. My mood is good my appetite is good also.

January 9, 2021, 3:44 PM

We had two powerful groups today, one talked about being re-covered and another talked about loving other people more than yourself. The other talked about grieving his mother's death. My mood is stable, and my psychiatrist changed my medicine. I take 250 mg of Depakote instead of 500 mg. I relapsed because I stopped going to meetings, stop calling my sponsor, stop reading, literature, etc. I lose my clean time, but I didn't practice don't pick it up it won't get in you. I even slept good last night.

January 12, 2021

I just came out of prayer it was OK. God 's eyes are over me and he hears my prayers. The group morning and afternoon was good. My appetite is wonderful. My meds are working well. We talked about relapse prevention and skills to cope with. Journaling is one way I cope. I called Towanda and she was shopping. She was enjoying herself. Shop until she dropped. She said that you are the winner because I was upset not seeing the Ravens play. My mood is stable. We had two croissants for breakfast and oatmeal. Juice and grapes. And salad. They gave us salads every day. My plan is to go to an outpatient to do something with my time. I am fearfully and wonderfully made. The group was full of the Spirit of God.

January 17, 2021

I am in treatment sitting on my bed. Just came from the bathroom. I had cravings for a cigarette today. Because I have been going out with smokers. Bad decision.

I remember before I went in I couldn't. I would be out with the smokers, and I picked my cigarette up. So, from now on I won't go out with the smokers. I had a good day; it was drama in the unit today. Another girl left today, but I am still here. I am glad I didn't act out on my thoughts to smoke. Smoking is bad news to me.

I slept good last night, and my mood is good, also my eating is good. My attitude is positive. Thank God for Jesus.

January 22, 2021, 6:50 AM

Sitting in the recreation room looking at the news. Today will be a good day. I took a shower this morning, took care of my hygiene. Boy was it a joy. Cleanliness is next to Godliness. God is a clean God, not dirty.

January 24, 2021

Today the unit was quiet. Lorrie and I got into an argument t because she provoked me to anger. My sponsor told me to be clothed with humility and to rebuke the devils in her.

We had the best lunch today, alfredo and salad. I enjoyed working with Kia. She is nice and humble. My friend will be leaving tomorrow. I sure will miss her. She is a blessing to me. I am getting in the shower now. Praise my mood is excellent.

January 25, 2021

I was thinking how you had a cigarette craving because my disease was active. The craving was strong and if I had gone outside I would have smoke, but God used Kia and I ran back into the door to come in to go upstairs. Now God revealed to me if that I pick up the cigarettes it will progress to the beer, to the marijuana, to the crack, to the prostitution, to the pan handling, to the lying, to the manipulation, to the spending all my money, etc.

I leave Feb 3rd. I am already prepared to go outside. I have all the information I need. I just need to practice it. I am not going to get any cleaner. The same information that they are the giving me on this program, they are telling me in all the treatment programs. All I must do is put staying clean first and have a plan for when I leave here. My plan is to go to an Outpatient Program, get a therapist and psychologist and do some voluntary work somewhere. I can go become a Peer Support Specialist. Dawn is concerned about me seeing Towanda. They want me to go in another programs, but I don't want to.

I will be doing it for them and not to be happy. I have changed my perspective on life. I know now that I can get enough of crack cocaine. I will never ever be satisfied if I start using again - one is too many and a thousand is never enough. That's how I know that I have surrendered to myself to the program. No more drugs. I can't have drugs and live. When I use, I lose. I want a life free from drugs. I want to live life on my God terms, no matter what. I am in the no matter club now. At first I couldn't say that. I can say aloud with conviction. I am in the no matter what club meaning whatever it takes by any means necessary.

I will follow the path and practice spiritual principles. I will no longer be complacent, which was my enemy toward spiritual principles I will no longer be indifferent toward spiritual principles. Neither will I allow people places and things who are not in recovery influence me to be diverted from my primary purpose. Not even the devil himself, even he I won't allow to divert me. I can't allow money and prosperity to divert me. Not a man, a job, or a father or jealousy or any other creature separate me from my recovery or God.

*God showed me that a was vigilance this time.

*That craving that I had eventually passed. And I told somebody I wanted to use cigarettes. To me cigarettes is a drug.

I will have tips to avoid relapse. I know I just can't have one. I am sick and tired of killing myself and abusing my body. Drugs kill and I am going to continue to pray as the doctor to delivers my dose of this psych meds. The only meds I will be on is my hypertension medicine and my sleep aids to help me sleep. I want to remove my body and mind from all drugs in order to recover. I don't view my relapse as a failure, but a jarring experience for a victorious application of the program.

Clean time speaks for itself:

12/12/2021   12/12/21
1/25/2021   12/25/21
1 year and 13-days   37 days
12 months = 1 year 1
13 days = I week and 6 days

January 26, 2021

I am sitting in my room on the bed, we have just come out from a meeting with Mrs. Kia. She loves the still suffering addict. Today I learned about stress and anger. If it is not dealt with it can cause me to use drugs. I am glad I have coping skills to deal with my stress and anger. I felt sleepy today because I stay up late last night. I fell asleep in group I felt drowsy. I know it was my medicine. They don't have any and maybe that's why I feel depressed and laid in my bed. My meditation is affective and paired with therapy. I need to be in social group with peers who participate in recovery free from substances. I need to be in a group in therapy led by a therapist. I need individual therapy.

My treatment plan:

- Individual therapy group therapy - led by a therapist, members encourage and support one another
- Support groups - meet with peers & support one another
- Medication - medication is most effective when paired with therapy

January 30, 2021, 12:50 PM

I am in The rock room in gardenia today. We just came from lunch. The menu was cold cut sandwich salad and soup, chips, and juice or iced tea. I received my medicine last night. I had good sleep last night. But before I had to suffer with some discomfort because I had to see the doctor in order to get refills. The lesson was to get a new psychiatrist or go back to the one I had. I never want to experience being without any of my meds. That is my trigger for me too used to self-medicate. So, what I did when I couldn't sleep I read about Job and Proverbs and did some step wk. We watch a movie about Omar who kept going to sell and kept relapsing. When I learned from the movie is he didn't want to put staying clean first.

I learned that drugs was just a symptom of my problem. My problem was me. I was the problem P my problem was that I have a disease of my feelings that I know very few much about and I have the most of. I realize that I must grow up emotionally and psychologically. I realize that my disease is mental, physical, and spiritual. I must treat them all in order to be complete. I must treat my disease through abstinence. My disease is only arrested. The old me is only arrested. I let her make bail. Using me as a whore, a thief, a liar, irresponsible, insensitive to people who love her, hurt her loved ones, reject those who are close to her. Panhandlers have entitlement issues. I was molested, hated to be poor, hated herself, stubborn, one of the more suffering. Lazy and live in their election from being homeless more than one home. Backslid more than one time and a hypocrite. Stayed clean, but lived dirty. Celebrity bogus anniversaries. Stole money from mother, sisters, teachers, and anybody I could steal from. Went to jail more than one time, lived in empty houses with boyfriend Vernon, ate at soup kitchens, spent my food stamps on drugs then beg to eat.

They're all **11 characteristics** of my disease:

1. Denial
2. Substitution
3. Rationalization
4. Justification
5. Distrust of others
6. Guilt
7. Embarrassment
8. Dereliction
9. Degradation
10. Isolation
11. Loss of control

What I learned about myself is that my depression can be a trigger and was a trigger for why I relapsed. Having feelings of inadequacies insufficient for purpose lacking the quality or quantity. Sometimes I don't feel like I have a meaning or purpose fully driven life. Some days I don't feel whole or complete. My strengths are my determination and virtuality and my positive thinking. My relationship with my higher is more than enough. But I am looking to be feeling normal. What is normal? What is the norm?

Memory Check
Reality Check

February 7, 2021, 5:00 PM

In the living room at my table:

Today I misplaced my phone. I was angry; I cried I was up. I feel better now because I'm going to buy another one. I'll pray over this one. I didn't pray over the boost phone that I had. That is why I lost it. I was not being vigilant or alert about it. Check on it everywhere I went. I lost it in the trucks I was going home and going to church. I can't explain why I lose keys and phones. God, please help me to have the ability to accept personal responsibilities. Thank you Jesus. This is the Super Bowl at 6 o'clock. I want Kansas to win. The sun is shining now. It snow today but it didn't stick. I took a shower this morning and took my medicine.

February 8, 2021, Monday 6:00 PM

I bought a new phone - it was exciting. I paid $85. What I learned was to keep focus and concentrate on important things. I talk to my therapist about me. What is low self-esteem? What is focus? What is concentration?

February 9, 2021, Tuesday 8:45AM

God woke me up at 8:45 AM, I took my meds first. I read my affirmations this morning.

February 20, 2021, 12:35 PM Saturday

I need to find a new sponsor. Me and Wanda broke up because she feels she can't help me anymore. I lied to her, and she was tired of me. She's not motivated me, so she thinks. She can't understand why I have changed since she has made me. But I disagree on how she wants me to go to Philadelphia for six months to a year. I'm not going into another treatment program. I'll listen to zoom meetings. Today is Ray's birthday. I'll not be going over to his house because he is using.

February 23, 2021, 1:35 AM Tuesday

Sitting at the dining room table. I just came up in prayer. I left want it and I feel relief because I have taken control over my own choices in my own life. I talked to Brother Aaron tonight. I made a conscious decision to go back to my old church to 2226 Park Ave. because God is leading me too. I just came upon prayer this morning. God really met me there. I cried out to God and spoke in my heavenly language. I asked him to give me a humble spirit and more of him and especially a clean heart to serve him. The spirit has a mind and it made intercession for me. It prays for me. Thank you Jesus!

I told Jesus I didn't want the riches of this land but that he would give me more of his love I told him to clean me up during this conservation that I am about to go on. So, I can be renewed spiritually. But I would walk after the spirit instead of the flesh. If God is for me, who can be against me? I feel pity for those who are against me! God will avenge me of all my enemies. My goal is to stay sober one day at a time and seek a skill for employment to take care of myself. Do some volunteer work somewhere.

Dawn encourage me today. I love her strength. She is my inspiration. Today is Tuesday. My plan is to spend the day with Jesus in his word and fasting. God give me wisdom to know the difference. Give me understanding of your gracious words of life. I would like to comment on nothing happens, you make it happen means I must put the work in order for it to happen. Whether it means a job, a marriage, promotion, etc. I must do the footwork in order for it to happen.

February 23, 2021, Tuesday 4 AM

I just came out of prayer. I thank God for bringing me out of that horrible pit called addiction. I thank Him for not letting the enemy swallow me up or destroy me. I'm in debt to Jesus I owe him. He paid for a debt I could not pay. It was his blood that brought my salvation or my deliverance not silver, gold, no money, but his precious blood that he shed and his resurrection that gives me the victory. Thanks be to God which gives me The victory. I will keep the TV off all this week until Monday, March 1, 2021. I can see clearly now that the rain is gone. All obstacles are out of my way. There's going to be a bright, bright sunshiny day. All around me are blue skies. Thank you universe. I am on a pink cloud, and I don't have to come down even when the storm comes again. I'll have peace in the midst of my storm. God or Jesus for universe or whatever is out there give Dawn peace until her storm passes. Hope she learns and grow from her challenges. If is persistent her a challenge, help her to learn from it and grow. Help her to know that she has a choice whether to let make her bitter or she has a choice to let it make her better. This is my prayer for her and myself. God you do hear an answer. What does the disease of addiction mean to me? How was your disease active recently?

- **Instant gratification** – *want to eat right now, don't want to wait*
- **Impatience** – *not wanting to be late and inability to be consistent* Sometimes not want to ask for help – *I have to humble myself and ask for help*
- **Gluttony**- Drinking energy drinks successfully/eating unhealthily

Step Work

First step: admit we were powerless over addiction and that our life has become unmanageable.

There are four questions:

1. **Can I control my use of drugs?** – Answer no control is not possible once it is suggested because my disease is progressive, incurable, and fatal if not arrested.
2. **Am I willing to stop using?** Definitely yes, with the help of the 12 steps and the sponsor from NA and other recovering addicts.
3. **Am I willing to do whatever it takes to recover?** Yes, even things I don't want to. I didn't want to go into treatment, but I went because my sponsor asked me to. Later, I found out that I need to be around other addicts who were doing what I was doing and get a firm foundation.
4. Given a choice between finding a new way of life in NA and continuing in our addiction recovery begins to appeal to us.

Conclusion: it is important to ask ourselves basic questions and step one (three)

1. Can I control my use of drugs?
2. Am I willing to stop using?
3. Am I willing to do whatever it takes to recover?
4. What are reservations? Those parts of outsells we won't surrender to the program.

Reservations can be anything; a belief that we can use a particular drug that we never had a problem with; placing a condition on our recovery, such as staying clean as long as our expectations are met; a belief that we can put into practice addicts; a belief that we can use again after a certain amount of clean time; working only certain steps – can't you spell conscious decision.

By keeping reservations, we are reserving a place in our program for relapse. My response was having an indifference, an attitude of indifference or intolerance towards spiritual principles. Not willing to change with my relapse. A feeling of inadequacy Dash feelings of self-pity. Still you need to do step work. I support work. Disconnecting from the source. Unplugging from my sponsors and recovering attic's. Not being vigilant meetings closed down. My depression was active. Got off my medicine. When I used my life grew worse.

1. Over what exactly am I powerless?

My dentures not coming from Florida when I want them to. I don't have control over the situation. I am powerless when a dentist clinic doesn't call me and tell me not to come out to the clinic because my dentures are not ready. I am powerless over people, places, and things. I can't control my using. I can't stop the progression.

2. One thing I did while in addiction that I never will do, and recovery is prostitution for panhandling – begging people for their money having oral sex with men. Some dirty penises. I won't eat out the trashcan in my recovery. I won't steal in recovery. I won't be sleeping in empty houses where no heat, no water, and no electricity occurs, and where rats and roaches live.

3. The things that I have done that went against my values and beliefs were having sex before marriage. Not bathing or showering. Not praying or stop praying. I lied and this goes against my beliefs. God hates a liar. All liars will have their part in the lake of fire and brimstone. Living in an empty house went against my beliefs. Living like an animal going to the bathroom outside went against my beliefs and values. I would shit and piss in a bucket in the empty house. Having sex and not married went against my beliefs and values. Stop praying and studying my word went against my values and beliefs.

4. My personality changes when I become self-centered. All I want is one more. I manipulate people, I lie, I steal and cheat. I don't care about my self-care. I don't take baths or showers. I don't be responsible over my life. I have responsibilities. I don't keep a phone, I lose keys, bus passes, etc. I don't concentrate or focus. I am not aware of my surroundings. I don't be alert or watchful. I have the cases of "fuck it." I don't feel the drugs and what they can do to me.

5. I tried to quit using on willpower, but it lasted only for a temporary time. I would stop using but couldn't say stop. I would stop for years then relapse. I have many bogus Anniversaries but never could stay for 10 steps. The only time I could really stop is when I ran out of money and drugs, and I still got a ways to get more money to use by tricky and panhandling I'm going into the stores and selling merchandise that I stole.

6. I would manipulate people by asking for money and say it is for food, but I would buy drugs with it. This was my manipulation. This is how I supported my use.

7. My addiction hurt myself by losing weight, burnt nose, guilt and shame and embarrassment. I hurt the people that loved me and cared about me, and I rejected the ones that loved me. I disappointed my family, but they didn't disown me.

God help me to stop destroying my life. God help me to change. Change my inconsistency. God help me to stop grieving. God help me to surrender to the program to the principles. God help me to stop using. I can use your power long before I understand. Going to a source of strength to me. I have a fear to live life. God help me to put trust in your power. My life used to be filled with distraction. I had to learn that I have a disease called addiction which was destruction in my life, and I am powerless over the destructive force. I learned that I need to find a force greater than my addiction. I have a power bigger than my addiction. God help me to allow my correction of life. Jesus Christ people in love. God didn't want me to have a dealership with the works of unfruitful darkness but rather come out from among them and be separate. But reprove them. Reprove my works of darkness and have no fellowship.

I am God's workmanship. God wants me to walk in good works. We are made to survive. Kind and pleasant, not harmful.

Friendship – emotions or conduct of friends
Mutual respect and support - state of being friends

Mutual affection- close friendships

When I am being honest about my feelings, it helps others to identify with me.

Honesty takes practice.

When I communicate honestly, each other. None of us should claim to be perfect. When we feel pressured or trapped it takes great spiritual and emotional strength to be honest. Keep working the steps. The program is when you live steps. Experience that you are going to gain time helps your ongoing recovery.

What shapes my personality?

The principles program my personality. We need a personality change. Where does my strength come from? Relationship with God of my understanding. Where does my hope and faith come from? People sharing the recovery to my relationship with the god of my understanding.

At first it feels awkward to share feelings. Part of the pain of addiction has been cut off from the shared experience.

Q: What do you do when you find yourself in a bad place or you have such trouble coming?
A: You call someone or go to a meeting. Going to see Caleb before making difficult decisions.

Q: How can you get through the toughest time?
A: By humbling yourself and asking for help. I can't, but **we** can.

Q: What helps recovering addicts stay clean?
A: Sharing regularly scheduled meetings.

Q: Why is it important to get a home group?

A: It is where people will get to know you. Provide encouragement from the people we get to know.

Q: What gives the addict a sense of joy?
A: Serving the members, the message – making ourselves available.

Q: What helps me to stay clean?
A: When I share comfort and encouragement with newcomers. When I should bring encouragement with others.

Q: How can I change?
A: By asking for help.

Q: What can be a barrier against change?
A: A closed mind. The way to find self-esteem is to help somebody find this new way of life.

Q: Who guides us?
A: Depending on a loving God who cares for us and will do for us what we find impossible to do for ourselves.

Ongoing recovery is very dependent on the wisdom from above:

1. **Pure** - no mixed or adulterated (free of contamination)
2. **Peaceable** - inclined to avoid argument or violent conflict.
3. **Gentle** - a mild king of tender temperament or character. not harsh or severe immoderate in action.
4. **Easy to be invented** - asking earnestly or anxiously to do something. to ask or beseech, implore, beg.
5. **No partiality** - favorable prejudice or bias. Being unfair prejudice in favor of or abundant living.
6. **No hypocrisy** - pretense. a person who pretends to have certain beliefs, attitudes, or feelings when they really do not.
7. **Full of mercy** - compassionate treatment having a capacity to forgive or showing kindness. giving someone a lighter punishment than they deserve.

8. Beta is the fruit of righteousness? Sown in peace of them that make peace. What is asking amiss? Asking for wrong motives.

The Tongue

My tongue defileth my whole body
It stains the whole body
The tongue is a little member; it boasts great things
My tongue is a fire
Everything in God's creature is tamed
What does tamed mean?
Submissive, docile
Teachable, easily managed or handled
Readily trained, teachable
Able to learn by being taught
My tongue is unruly
Disorderly, disruptive, no control, or discipline
Using punishment to correct disobedience

No man can tame the tongue
Full of deadly position
Life and death are in the power of the tongue
My words can speak life or speak death
My tongue can build others up or tear them down
Not submissive or conforming to rule
Ungovernable, turbulent, lawless

Endure

- Weeping may endure for a night, but joy cometh in the morning. *Psalms 30:5*
- Goodness of God endures continually *Psalm 52:1*
- God's truth endure to all generations *Psalm 100:5*
- Thou mercy endures for every *Psalm 138:8*
- I am going to be hated by all man for his namesake, but yet I endure unto the end I shall be saved *Matthew 10:22*
- He that shall endure unto the end the same shall be saved
- *Matthew 24:13*
- Love endures all things *1 Corinthian 13:7*
- For the time will come when they will not endure sound doctrine. They will turn their ears from the truth and be turned into fables 2 *Timothy 4:3*
- If ye endure chastening; God dealt will you as with His sons. The chastening wasn't joyous, as a matter of fact, it was grievous, but afterward, it yields the peaceable fruits of righteousness. *Hebrews 12:7*

He is me Father of spirits and life. I became a partaker of his holiness. A person who leaves home and live recklessly and who spends money in a recklessly extravagant way. I wasted my substances with righteous living I came to myself.

Opponent -foe-enemy-rival; person who brings harm or danger. Oppression

March 31, 2021

Amekia and I had a disagreement today. I allowed her to get off the phone. I learned that I must be meek even when people are saying things that I may disagree with. We can learn to agree to disagree. I must remain teachable. Be humble and ask God to help me to succumb unto him, resist the devil and he shall flee. I still love her, but sponsorship is a two-way street.

April 5, 2021

It is now one o'clock in the morning. I was on the phone with Aaron. God has blessed our relationship and friendship. God orchestrated this relationship, not my flesh but the spirit allowed him to come in my life. He has been a true friend and a godly man of God. He is a good teacher.

I don't praise him, but I do praise him when I am led to by God. God said don't praise yourself, let another man praise you. I am going to a meeting this morning at 7;20. It is God's permission. If he allows me, I will do so and so. I have N.A. N.A. can help me. Thank God for relief. I talked to Renee. She thought that I stole something, but it was revealed to me that I didn't. I felt relieved.

I was ready to repent and confess. I was ready for my punishment that I was praying for somebody. God revealed to me that he smote me in his wrath but with his mercy and favor he delights. I was forsaken and hated. I am the work of his hands. He opened my personal house. A crown of glory in the theme hand and a royal kinship in the hand of the Lord. He told me the delightful in me because I study in His word.

The watchmen are upon the walls. That they shall never hold their peace day or night. Keep not silent. God wants me to be a praise in the earth. God told me he will not give my soul to be meat for thine enemies. In my affliction, he was afflicted in his love and his compassion. He redeemed me. He carried me all the days of my life. I rebelled and vexed his holy spirit; therefore, he turned to be my enemy and he fought against me. The way of a transgressor is hard. We are the holy people.

Hosea 14:4–9

"I will heal their waywardness
  and love them freely,
    for my anger has turned away from them.
5 I will be like the dew to Israel;
  he will blossom like a lily.
Like a cedar of Lebanon
  he will send down his roots;
6   his young shoots will grow.
His splendor will be like an olive tree,
  his fragrance like a cedar of Lebanon.
7 People will dwell again in his shade;
  they will flourish like the grain,
they will blossom like the vine—
  Israel's fame will be like the wine of Lebanon.
8 Ephraim, what more have I[c] to do with idols?
  I will answer him and care for him.
I am like a flourishing juniper;
  your fruitfulness comes from me."

9 Who is wise? Let them realize these things.
  Who is discerning? Let them understand.
The ways of the Lord are right;
  the righteous walk in them,
  but the rebellious stumble in them.

God healed my soul. He turned his anger away from me. He loves me freely. He harkens unto me. I will grow as the lily for his ways of righteousness and the just shall walk in them. But the transgressors shall fall therein. My help is in God. God experiences rejection. They wanted a King to reign over them instead of God.

April 10, 2021, 8:10

Whathat are you thankful for? I am thankful for the gift of recovery; gift of the Holy Ghost; gift of life; gift of prayer; gift of health, gift of food and drink; gift of a roof over my head; gift of a bed to sleep on; a bathroom and shower; gift of godliness and righteousness; gift of wisdom, wealth, and riches; gift of a sound mind.

I will learn contentment by being or having godliness. Being godly is great. Gift of breath.

April 14, 2021

Today is my spiritual birthday.

This is the day I made a great decision to turn my will and my life over to the will of God. As I understand him. Deacon Bruce Edwards opened up the church on 2226 Park Ave on a Monday night. I tarried around the altar until I was enduring with power from on high. It suddenly came as a mighty rushing wind and filled my house. I spoke in the heavenly language of tongues. Jesus was in my mind, but God got a hold of my tongue, and he took over and spoke through me. It was an experience that I've never had before. I truly repented and I didn't have anyone to tell me I got it. I heard myself speak. After all these years I still speak when the Holy Ghost takes over only I can interpret. Sometimes what I am saying. He only reveals to me what I am saying. The interpretation of tongues. The Holy Ghost is a gift that says not to forbid to speak in it.

I have changed my mind many times. I took my will back. I have done things, said things, I shouldn't have said. In other words, I have fell short many times in his glory, but he never forsook me or left me. He is here with me right now. He was merciful to my unrighteousness. I paid for my sins because every sin and disobedience shall receive a just recompense of reward. The same way he rewards me for my righteousness, he chastens me sure for my sins and the way of transgressors is hard.

He that soweth sparingly shall reap also sparing king and he with soweth bountifully shall reap also bountifully. *2 Corinthians 9:6*

Be not deceived, God is not mocked; for whatsoever a man soweth, that shall he also reap. *Gal 6: 7-9*

Job 28

Where does wisdom live?
Where is the place of understanding?

It is not found in the land of the living?
The dept saith it is not found in me
The sea saith it is not with me

Gold cannot equal without it
Gold, silver, and crystal cannot equal it
Coral, or pearls- the price of wisdom
Is above rubies
It cannot be valued without pure gold

Where does wisdom cometh from?
Where is the place of understanding

Wisdom is hidden from eyes of all
Living and kept close from the fowls of the air

Death and destruction heard of the fame thereof

With our ears Verse 23 [(Job 28:23)]

God knows and understands where it lives- he knows the place thereof. He (God) sees under the whole heaven. He make ways for the wind and weighs the water by measure.

If we diligently seek something face, we shall find it. God is a rewarder of them that diligently seek him. Without faith, it is impossible to please Him. He responds to our faith – He moves by our faith. Jesus did not succumb, rather He resisted each temptation. He walked the path of pain utilizing God's word as our guide. Being steadfast in all your ways means being firm in belief, determination, or adherence. The way to know that you are following God's plan for your life is being in prayer. Take time each day to devote yourself to the Lord and the plans He has for your life.

Being grounded means being anchored and hold on in spite of storms, winds, and rain. An anchored heart posture that lets us stand when trouble comes. Rooted is fixed in one position, immobile, unable to move grounded not allowed to fly. He speaks in terms of peace not anxiety. No matter the source of our heartbreak, Lord, you can heal the brokenhearted and bind up the wounds.

Fixed in one position immobile unable to move.

Galatians 6:9
Be not weary in well doing for we shall reap if we faint not.

1 Cor 15:58
Therefore steadfast, unmovable, and always abounding of the work of the Lords. Nothing is in vain when boundaries are lower chaos comes. Falling out full of where you come from than being in the present moment. Disdain and rejection. Laugh him out of the synagogue. You can't survive but it costs me nothing.

Faith in a crisis
John 20: 25-26

Not written in this book. Great skepticism in this time. Believe in something so prevailing that doubt is running wild. Don't believe in science or God. Blindness make people comfortable in their zone. We pray to the things instead of God. We used to believe in a constitution in which preaching is based on faith. No parents, order, etc. and no structure and not safe with a contract. Unbelievers don't believe – Unbelief is evil. The world is talking about church not deliverance. It must be revealed.

John 3:14
Believe in Him.

Carried away with every wind of doctrine
Faith is the currency of God
An exchange
Lack of faith insults God
A friend of God
Importance of faith
Would he find faith on earth?
Death was not in their plan or understanding
I will go and die with him
Why should I stay?
God left
He saved others but won't save himself
Thomas was not in the room when
Jesus came
That his faith fail you not
Promise
Talk loyal; when you're up
Much learning has made you mad
Child-like Faith
Joseph Arimathea

God left the ninety-nine to get the lost one. You are important un-to Him. He shows up for the unbeliever. The cost of discipleship is a cross. Following Him is not cool. You can be touch how I feel. God can stand for you to get on His nerves. An ambassador. Touch me in my wounded place. I will show you

January 2, 2022

Dear Jesus,

Jesus told tonight that he shall not rest unto his righteousness go as brightness. God's word tells us in *Isaiah 62:1-5* that

For Zion's sake I will not keep silent,
for Jerusalem's sake I will not remain quiet,
till her vindication shines out like the dawn,
her salvation like a blazing torch.
2 The nations will see your vindication,
and all kings your glory;
you will be called by a new name
that the mouth of the Lord will bestow.
3 You will be a crown of splendor in the Lord's hand,
a royal diadem in the hand of your God.
4 No longer will they call you Deserted,
or name your land Desolate.
But you will be called Hephzibah,[a]
and your land Beulah[b];
for the Lord will take delight in you,
and your land will be married.
5 As a young man marries a young woman,
so will your Builder marry you;
as a bridegroom rejoices over his bride,
so will your God rejoice over you.

Thou anointed my head with oil of gladness above thy fellows. Thou loves righteousness and hates wickedness. The King greatly desires thy beauty for he is thy Lord and worships through him. I am a King's daughter. All glorious. My clothing is of pure gold. I am a prince in all the earth. God hates robbery for burnt offering and loves judgment. I will greatly rejoice in thee. God showed me that the upright love him. We remember his love more than wine. What I learned from my backsliding is that God allowed me to fight, stay in the fight and he used my cross to his glory. I swung even when I didn't feel like swinging.

Prophetess- female prophet

1. **Miriam**   Exodus 15: 20-21
2. **Deborah**   Judges 4:4-5
3. **Hilkiah**   2 Kings 22: 12-20
4. **Isaiah's Wife**   Isa 8: 1-3
5. **Anna**   Luke 2: 36
6. **Daughters of Phillip** Acts 2: 8-9
7. **Prophecy**
   Concerning   Joel 2: 28

Dear Jesus,

Greetings, blessed Lord, my king, my prince, my high tower, my kings men redeemer, my rose of Sharon, my bright and morning star, my sweet savior, my sword. The reasons all these praise coming out because God has won himself the victory once again. I knew he would defeat Goliath and cut his head off. I knew he would lift up a standard against the enemy. He drowned him in the Red Sea, and I walked on dry ground. His right arm hath gotten him the victory. With an outstretched arm hath he gotten himself glory and praise and honor one more time. He is allowing me to walk in my destiny, my calling.

He called me for His purpose and for His plan. It's no longer my will but His will be done; not mine. Satan pursued me today and God turned and pursued or chased him. He tried to block me from hearing the world of God from Chad today. Tactics- but God casted him out. I told him he was a loser. He bluffed me but I called him bluff. My legs were paining me, but I anointed my feet, and I evicted the pain. I talked to the pain. I told the pain that you can't live here. You got to go- leave, right now. I gave an order, and I commanded the devil to leave, and he left. I am his witness. I prayed for god to send a planter and me giveth increase. I witnessed to a girl called Linda.

I thanked God for His crushing because through his crushing, He made new wine in new bottles. The wine is the Holy Ghost. I thanked God for my pain because my pain brings power. I thanked God for my sufferings because pressure bring the anointing and power. After I suffered awhile, He perfected me, established me, grounded me, and settled me. I learn of God when I walk through the shadow of the valley of death. I didn't fear no evil. I took a licking and kept on ticking. What I learned tonight was through all I went through, nothing can or no one or nobody or no demons can cause me to be taken out of God's hand. He planted me. All of my problems, sufferings, hardships, and adversities brought me closer to God. God showed me the parable of the rich fool. He told me that He has a storehouse that he is going to pen up unto me and to be rich towards him. I am rich in God. The blessings of God maketh the rich and added no sorrow. I am ready this year to walk in my destiny and potential. After the Holy Ghost is come upon you, ye shall have power. He told me not to set my affection on earth beneath buy lay my treasures in heaven.

He had a plan even though I had pain. My pain was God's purpose He uses. A rose not only have flowers but thorns. The Lord stood with me that is why I came back. He was standing with me even when I wasn't standing with him. His fruit was sweet to my taste. His banner over me was love. I am sick of love. Godliness with contentment is great gain. Bloom where you are planted. His voice. It was good that I was afflicted. Leaping and skipping upon the hills denotes my dance for him. I was delivered from the lion's mouth. I used and could have died of AIDS. You can imitate my steps but not my gratitude. The lions had me in their mouth, but God delivered me.

God will rescue me from every evil attack. My confidence is in Him. I will not cast my confidence away. I had to accept God's plan over my own life. I have accepted the course that God has for me. You can't win by not being confident in your equipment. You are good with what God gave you. Fear was feeding you. You didn't get it on earn double for trouble. The rain is gone for a season. One pain is over. We are positioned on purpose. He planted Nehemiah there.

God's desire is toward His church. What do you want? **The hand of God is on me**. God is going to use other people to bless you. Never let Satan's wall define boundaries that only God can defend.

January 3, 2022, 10:10pm

Dear Jesus,

I thank you for today, Jesus. You let me get rest. You let me pay my rent. You let me pay my debt. I sang songs to Jesus- He loves singing. Come before me with singing. I make a joyful noise to Him. He allowed me to eat a salad and salmon. God, you are a great provider. Jehovah Jireh. You are a present help in time of trouble. My trouble or my blessings are that this pain and affliction and the medicine isn't working. Many are the afflictions of the righteous, but the Lord is going to deliver me from them all.

This pain is my purpose. God has a plan for me. He is working behind the scenes. We are works in progress. When we are close to our destiny, all hell breaks loose that's why I said to God get all the glory. Great things He has done. We need to trust Him and respect Him. We get in the lion's den, but God tames their mouth. We are in the fiery furnace, but God is in it with us. He purges us and refines us. We are chosen in the furnace of affliction. We have mental attacks and physical too.

God broke my stubbornness and rebellious spirit. For stubborn is witchcraft and rebellion is idolatry. Real worship is sacrifice. God have me victory today. Although I am in the lion's den and in the fiery furnace, *I have on the whole armor of God.* **The whole armor helps me to stand. I withstand the fiery darts.** God sent His angel today to touch my eyes so I can read and write. I kept reading the bible and putting it down. But when my help came, the devil had to flee. He flees when we yield to the authority of God.

God has blessed me to overcome many obstacles. The psych medicine is not working. My steps have been on hold, but God is restoring me. He heal my backsliding. He took my bad and used it for my good. He used my abuse to make me strong. All that I went through is what Jesus went through. He was forsaken, abused, persecuted, homeless, poor, etc. He helped me to address issues, or my issues would address me. God didn't let Satan's weapons form to prosper.

January 5, 2022

D<small>ear Jesus,</small>

Thank you for waking me up. Thank you for the bus pass. He allowed me to find $20.00 in my pocketbook to pay for my bus pass. He proved to me that He will supply all my needs according to His riches in glory. Thank you, Jesus, for Antonette. God used her to give me $40.00. I took $20.00 tom wash my clothes. God told me not to be made at Correy but love him and pray for him. I was in the lion's spirit, and he took me from the flame, from the fire- it didn't burn me. He quenched the fire. Tracey took me to dinner and bought me a book. It is a good book about fear and anxiety. God helped me to wash my clothes. I threw some things away today, took a shower and brushed my teeth. God helped me in my challenges. You are better than your problems. It is not power, not by mine but God keeps His word.

January 10, 2022

Dear Jesus,

I am thankful to you because you visited me in prayer and worship tonight. I cried because of some of the praise songs I learned. I am His favored. He delights and honors me. No pain today. Fasting yes. I gave up the manna for Jesus. He will reward me when I diligently seek Him. I chase after him. I'm royalty and am an ambassador- His representative on earth, His masterpiece, His trophy, and His jewel. I've been chosen in the furnace of affliction. Refined in the fire as silver is refined and gold. I am His masterpiece. He took His time on me. He keeps blowing my mind. Never thought He would take my failures to His glory to work together for my good. He released my chains and shackles. He turned my captivity- my slavery. Now I'm his slave. Now I'm his prisoner. He's my guardian. My bodyguard, my protector, my husband, my kinsmen, redeemer, my first love. He is Holy. His grace makes me worthy.

February 21, 2022

Dear Jesus,

Today was a sunny day. The sun was bright and shiny just like my spiritual life. In church, Sunday, God came through breaking our physical and emotional yokes. My arm and back was severe pain, but God broke the chains that had me in brutal pain. This pain has a purpose. It serves me to pray harder. If I didn't have it, I wouldn't pray. Chad preached the strength of prayer. The power of prayer. I broke my fast today, but that's ok. I'll do the meeting tomorrow on the second STEP. God, please use me. Here am I.

Dear Jesus,

God gave me permission to get up. To get up from losing my friend, Aaron. Although I lost him, I didn't lose my friend that sticks closer than a brother who is Jesus. Though I lost him, I didn't lose my courage. I got tired of hurting others. When I cast my care upon the Him, all my care he took it and cast it in the lake of fire. I believe in God and not my feelings. My feelings had to change through my walk. There is life in the power of the tongue. Death and life is in the power of the tongue. Pettiness destroys purpose over his pettiness. Had to trust new people to trust somebody new. So cynical. Bring somebody who knows when the treasure as.

March 1, 2022

Dear Jesus,

Jesus tested today and He revealed to me that he was guarding my money. Protected my money from hackers. He tested me today, but gave me the victory. My name is victory. He is amazing to me. Today was a fast day. Me and Stephanie went to Crafty Crab, a seafood place. She was so happy. She is my true friend. She taught me how to be a true friend. My friend, Aaron, died but I am no longer hurting. God has lifted that burden.

March 6, 2022

Dear Jesus,

Today God woke me up on time. I slept well. Thank God for forgiving me for much. Therefore I praise Him for much. He stopped the devil from killing me. He stopped HIV and He stopped cancer and depression from conquering me. I love you, Jesus! Chad told me I reminded him of Sister Banning. She loved the word, and His word and Spirit is my treasure. That is where my heart is.

March 18, 2022, 9:30pm

Dear Jesus,

Listening to Bible Enrichment tonight. It was about standing with the whole armor. God blessed me with $25.00. I gave Him $2.50. But I will be a good steward over my finances. Troy stayed at Light Group while I went to Dee's place. He shared a good meeting. Jeff always share a good meeting. Mrs. Houston called me while I was in therapy- my meetings are my therapy. For the therapeutic, meetings are one addict helping another addict.

March 20, 2022, 12:10pm

Dear Jesus,

Thank you for new mercies this day. Thank you for this lesson that I learned, Jesus, that you taught me. The fire alarm went off after I came in yesterday or last night. It was so loud that I began to rebuke it, but it was not the devil that had it loud. It was God trying to teach me a lesson. So when it didn't go off when I rebuked it, then I said the God will allow it to go off when He is ready. But I was in prayer, and I didn't get up until I couldn't stand the sound. I shut my door and got down on my face and prayed again. Then the Spirit spoke to me that tribulation produces patience, but patience has to have its own work that ye might be complete. When I surrendered, the sound went off because I surrendered. I admitted complete defeat. I had to apply step one to the situation.

I was powerless over that sound, but I could surrender to my higher power and pray. And that's why He sent Him. I did try to put my hand in it because I place something up there against the noise. But

then I practices my program steps and used prayer and my higher power mediation and surrendered to the steps. It worked for me. N.A. works but you must apply the steps or a step to your situation. I must surrender to my higher power. I must humble myself to Him so He can help me. My help comes from Him, and this God-sent program called N.A. Thank you God.

March 28, 2022

Those that were under Moses's law died without mercy under two or more witnesses. Israel made a calf of gold. Moses made them drink it God plagued the people for their sins. It is better for God to know you. Some people that say they know God, but God doesn't know them. Without His Spirit, you are none of his. Many will say that they know God. Didn't we cast out devils in your name? Did we not speak in tongues? Depart from me ye worker of iniquity.

The Lord forgave me tonight for my backbiting and lying. If I confess my sins, He is just and faithful to forgive me and He cleansed me when I went down in prayer tonight. He met me in tongues. My heavenly language I spoke. He gave me $30.00 today. We had a church meeting today. God didn't give me ideas until after I came home. And I prayed on my knees. I like the way god lead me to read His word and gave me a mind to read. A mind and what to read. He lead me and I read about the tongue. How it is unruly deadly poison. **It can be tamed.**

April 5, 2022, 11:45pm

Tonight me and Troy talked on the phone. God lead me to pray tonight. He was listening while I was talking. I am not a mistake or an accident. He gave me an understanding of powerlessness. A form of surrender in saying, "I am an addict". I can't stay on my own. Second admission. I can't control my using [drugs]. I can't recover without honesty, open mindedness, willingness. There is a seed that is in me. With God, I'll nourish it.

April 21, 2022

Dear Jesus,

The Lord lead me to apply for college- CCB. Jeff influenced me. I had difficulties but God helped me to persist. God met us in prayer. Chad gave a word of knowledge and a word of wisdom. The Spirit met me in prayer in my bed. I cleaned my apartment. I found that I have my credits. I want to go to school for the rest of my life. I want to be used by God anytime and anywhere. We are going to PA. Me and Antonette went to the gym. God touched my back. Thank you   Jesus.

April 23-26, 2022

Dear Jesus,

April 23rd, me, and Antonette went to Pennsylvania. The drive was 3 to 4 hours long. When we go there after the baseball game, we got left and we couldn't find our way. Then I told Maria, "let's pray". We were in spiritual warfare, but God gave us the victory. My goddaughter, ReRe, has a beautiful family; she and Michael love and support their family. Mandy was very fun and loveable to be around.

Josiah was a champion. I kept telling him. Alexis and her brother needed discipline, but we loved them in spite of them not having manners and respect. Their mom was young. Maria cleaned her floors and told her to clean her house. We stayed over Lil's house- it was clean. I slept in her bed. We celebrated Mannie's birthday in church. He was prayed over and the family. Renee' Michael's mother was there.

She was sweet and she talked with us the whole way through. Today, April 26th, I missed Meagan because I was at my meeting. The subject was a *Full Life in NA*. God lead me to be on the phone handling my FSA's business. I have to get a new access code for them to get my old username and password. The job was tedious. God lead me home to wash my small load of clothes. I play Pokeno and missed four corners. I only played $3 just to be sociable with the seniors in the building. Nobody was using profanity or bad spirits wasn't lurking.

Today at Light Street, I saw Troy and they were reading the Ninth Tradition. N.A. is not organized- no managers or supervisors or governments.

April 30, 2022

Dear Jesus,

God let me get in to school. He moved my fear by helping me to replace it with faith and confidence in Him. I can do all things through Christ which strengthens me. With His help, I'm going all the way to school to a Ph.D. degree. Diane can help me since she finished school. He , (Jesus) is my motive for and supplier of my needs. He will supply me with the finances. He didn't let me enter in to not find me the Pell Grant. Thank you Jesus. Today is Tracey's birthday. Yesterday, we went to *Helping Up Mission*. She spend it with her family. We went to *Helping Up Mission's* meeting.

May 1, 2022

Dear Jesus,

Today is Scott's birthday. Happy birthday Scott. Tracey's is Sunday, the Lord's day. Service was great. The Lord surprised me. I though my phone would be turned off until Monday, but Tracey paid for it through her credit card. I praised and thanked God in prayer. I believe He will work out my financial problems also. It is already done. He told me, *"I can't work until you give me your faith"*.

May 12, 2022, 10:35pm

Dear Jesus,

Today I lost my bus pass. I've been losing things lately. But I recognized my attitude. I've been trusting God that He will fix it. He gave me blessed assurance today. In prayer, He met me. I took a shower with my Dove body wash. I was reading 2 Cor 4:7-11 and 16 through 18. God wants me to rely on His treasure which the Holy Spirit that the power may be of Him and not of me. He is faithful that's promised. Another bus pass is going to show up; you just wait and see. I know God can't fail but I fail.

May 17, 2022

Dear Jesus,

The Lord allowed to see another birthday. I spend in Dee's 7:30 to 8:30 meeting. Then I came home and prepared myself for the next meeting. God met us there and we felt His power. Tracey said the closing prayer. It was Edwin's 25th anniversary. He was a humble servant. I'll be speaking out there on May 26th on a Thursday. Darlene Graves was there. I love her Spirit. I was full when I came home. My cup was running over because God really use me as His vessel. I truly was fulfilled. He has filled all the places in me.

He has made me whole. I am complete in Him. The fullness of the Godhead body is fulfilled in Jesus. God prepared a body for himself to dwell in Mary. He overshadowed her.

How do I feel? What are some of my emotions I've been experiencing.

I've been feeling empowered.
Like a champion, like an overcomer,
like a victor.

If God be for me, who can be against me. He has destroyed my foes; they can't defeat me. He has torn down my mountains by my faith. He has killed my giants and torn down my Jericho walls. He fulfilled my dreams. He helped me to forget about my past. Because I am blessed, my family is blessed. I feel the flow of His love going through me. This is just the beginning of God using me. He has a great work for me to do. Signs, miracles, and healings shall follow them that believe. I am going to branch out into the deep. I will go from glory to glory.

About the Author

Antonette Brown currently resides in Baltimore, Md. She is a new writer and author, and a devout biblical scholar. She enjoys attending worship services at her church near her home fellowshipping with the outreach ministry. Brown still attends group recovery therapy weekly and often provides her testimony of how she is becoming an heir of the promises of God. She loves to travel, read inspirational books, discuss politics, and enjoys watching sports. She aspires to return to complete her degree at Towson University.

References

1. Scriptures retrieved from http://www.biblegateway.com

2. Narcotics Anonymous: https://www.narcotics.com/na-meetings/maryland/baltimore/

Notes

www.ingramcontent.com/pod-product-compliance
Lightning Source LLC
Chambersburg PA
CBHW070303290526
45791CB00003B/1070

Weisman, Steven R. 30 January 2005. "Under Pressure, Qatar May Sell Jazeera Station" New York: The New York Times. Late Edition, Final, Sec. 1, Col. 3, Pg. 1.

Williams, Daniel. 13 October 2001. "Al-Jazeera Ascends to World Stage: Bin Laden Tape Brings Notice to Arab Station" Washington: *Washington Post*. A22. <www.washingtonpost.com/ac2/wp-dyn/A52278-2001Oct12>

Wolton, Dominique. 2003. *L'autre mondialisation*. Paris: Flammarion.

Younge, Gary and Vikram Dodd. June 29, 2005. "CIA blunder on al-Jazeera 'terror messages.'" London: *The Guardian*. Guardian Home Pages 3.

Zayani, Mohamed. 2005. "Introduction—Al Jazeera and the Vicissitudes of the New Arab Mediascape." In Zayani, Mohamed. *The Al Jazeera Phenomenon: Critical Perspectives on New Arab Media*. Boulder, CO: Paradigm Publishers.

Zednik, Rick. 2002. "Inside Al-Jazeera." *Columbia Journalism Review*. 40.6: 44-7.